Nonfiction, Memoir, or Fiction?

Dissecting the Works
Of Laura Ingalls Wilder

A Critical Paper Submitted to
the Faculty of the Creative Writing Program
at Ashland University, Ohio
in Partial Fulfillment of the Requirements
for the Degree of Master of Fine Arts.

By

Robynne Elizabeth Miller

ISBN: 1-947370-04-9
ISBN-13: 978-1-947370-04-3

DEDICATION

To all those who love old things and old ways.

And to those who allow me to love them, too.

.

CONTENTS

ACKNOWLEDGMENTS

This paper was written as part of the MFA
requirements for my Masters Degree in
Creative Nonfiction and Fiction
from Ashland University in Ashland, Ohio.
It combines my interest in pioneer literature,
particularly the works of Laura Ingalls Wilder,
and my fascination with hybrid genres.

I am grateful to my professors, Robert Root and
Erika Krouse for their help in shaping my ideas
into a cohesive concept and for allowing me
to explore my literary interests and passions.

INTRODUCTION

Few American authors have produced a significant body of multi-genre work which has then spawned a vast amount of biographical and historical documentation corroborating (or disputing) that work. Laura Ingalls Wilder, however, is one of those authors. Because of this rare convergence, Wilder offers a glimpse into the complexities of semi-autobiographical prose. In her writing, a unique combination of autobiography, in the form of creative nonfiction, memoir, and pure fiction resides. But what distinguishes truth from fiction? Where do the lines between them blur? Why did Wilder choose to combine the genres at all? And how does it affect our understanding of her story?

It's important to consider that a writer makes an implied contract with a reader when defining their work. By making a statement about the fundamental nature of a story, the writer is inviting expectations. If a book is labeled "fiction," for example, readers look for a made up story, a hero's journey of some kind, and an antagonist. If it's memoir, on the other hand, they look for a personal interpretation of, and response to, an event or situation in the writer's past. They expect the account to be true, but also consider the issue of subjectivity inherent in such a reflection. With autobiography, however, readers expect a high level of objective truth. Even when creative nonfiction allows some flexibility with dialog, etc., it's anticipated that the work is inherently accurate. Nothing added. Nothing excluded which would intentionally alter our understanding of the story. No factual details changed to suit some larger purpose.

But what happens when a "hybrid genre" appears? What happens when elements of two or more genres emerge in one piece of writing? What is the contract, then?

In the writing of her family's history, Wilder made a categorical statement that her stories were "literally true, names, dates, places, every anecdote and much of the conversation are historically and actually true. (Wilder qtd. in Anderson 247) But we know now, from a variety of sources, including her own words, that this was not accurate. So, why did she combine genres?

Did she embellish and massage the truth because she didn't foresee either the internet's future reach or the interest (and analysis) her works would garner? Because of this inability to predict modern research options and the way her work would eventually be scrutinized, did she simply think she would "get away with" blending truth and fiction? Or did she deeply feel that the blending of genres was both acceptable and necessary in the telling of the greater pioneer story? If the latter, why did she slip over the line of creative nonfiction/fiction into the realm of memoir? Memoir is so personal and subjective, and not typically found in straight nonfiction or in fiction. Why, then, did she feel the need to blend all of these genres in one over-arching story?

It's true that Wilder's ability to weave narratives from such varied perspectives is intriguing in itself. But more important than the "how" is the "why" of that weaving. That is what this paper seeks to discover. By teasing out and dissecting portions of her work which represent the varied genres of nonfiction, memoir, and fiction, I will explore how and why Wilder chose to write each portion of her books in the particular manner she did, and discover how each genre and subgenre influenced and informed each other.

In doing so, we'll discern what she gained or lost in making those narrative choices, what the impact her choices made on the series' narrative arc as a whole, and whether this decision to combine seemingly disparate literary techniques was successful.

BACKGROUND

Laura Ingalls Wilder (1867-1957) was a prolific, award-winning American writer, active from 1911-1943. She has sold over one hundred million copies of her books in more than sixty countries. Wilder is most famous for her *Little House on the Prairie* series of eight books, with one further book (*The First Four Years*), not initially intended to be part of the series, published posthumously. The books are typically marketed as autobiographical creative nonfiction, but Ms. Wilder began her career as a magazine columnist for the *Missouri Ruralist,* and wrote many newspaper articles, as well. Before the *Little House* series was even conceived or began, Wilder had long established herself as a popular and productive journalist and essayist.

After her death at the age of ninety, and as interest in both the books and the author's legacy continued to grow, collections of Wilder's essays, articles, and personal letters were published and heavily annotated. This gave the public an unprecedented glimpse into not only what and when she wrote, but also how and why. Further research conducted by fans of Wilder, and fans of America's history of westward migration, has deepened our understanding of the environment, culture, and even specific characters she was writing about.

It is likely that Wilder never expected or imagined the enduring popularity of her books. Nor could she have fathomed the resulting intense interest in her personal life, correspondence, or initial writing drafts. And, of course, there is no way she could have envisioned a time when a thing called "the internet" would render historical research almost instantaneous and fact-checking relatively easy. This non-expectation is important. It makes studying Wilder a rare and unique opportunity. She never expected her writing to be dissected or corroborated or thoroughly examined in any way. This means that she wrote without the expectation of anyone ever looking over her shoulder, questioning her motives, or checking her facts. She simply wrote in a way she believed served the story she wanted to tell. But with a combination of her non-expectation of scrutiny as she wrote and our modern-day access to volumes of verifiable documentation, we can not only discern where fiction and nonfiction crossed in her work, but also begin to unravel why it ever crossed at all.

Robynne Elizabeth Miller

PREMISE

Before we begin, it's important to establish the premises we are working under. The first premise is that "genre" is important. A quick look at BISAC codes (Book Industry Subject and Category codes) reveals approximately one hundred and fifty fiction genres alone. Why so many? Partially for the publisher, who needs clear descriptions and categories under which they can market the book. Partially, it's because the reader wants to know what the book contains, i.e.: the implied contract mentioned above.

The second premise is that, for the purposes of this exploration, we will divide Wilder's writing into three categories: Nonfiction, Memoir, and Fiction. Nonfiction refers to writing that is factually true, even if it is presented in a creative nonfiction format. Traditionally, memoir is a subset of the greater genre of nonfiction. For our purposes, however, it's important to separate it out. Memoir is that which is factually true, but also contains introspection and emotional interpretation. Fiction is writing which is completely made up.

The third premise is that Wilder was not entirely accurate in defining her own work. She frequently described her *Little House* series as true stories about her childhood. Modern research and the discovery of Wilder's own letters and writing notes, however, suggest that she employed a combination of techniques in the crafting of her books, which render them more accurately described as a complex combination of nonfiction, memoir, and fiction . . . a hybrid genre.

WHY IS GENRE IMPORTANT?

Prolific novelist, Cathy Yardley, in an article entitled "Why Genre Matters," stated that "the true beauty of genre is to work within the structure, to fulfill the reader's expectations and natural storytelling rhythms . . . and yet do so in a way that not only follows the form, but still manages to create true surprise, engagement, and tension. . . ." For Yardley, genre is clearly a safe place in which to meet the reader's expectations and also a solid form upon which creativity and literary exploration can rest.

With a similar view on the import of genre, actress and author Dinah Lenney told of a meeting she once had with another writer:

> He was determined to school us: we should put our attention on the work, not the genre. What's the diff? he asked. What, indeed? I wondered afterwards: if there's no diff, why make a deal of it? Why distract me, why not be straightforward? What if he'd told us instead: I'll start with an essay; I'll end with a poem; I'll read you a story in the middle — would that have interfered with his enjoyment or mine? Or might it have allowed me to

focus, not on the pretense, but on the prose? (Lenney et al.)

Lenney is asking an important question here: Does the concept of genre allow us to focus on the work, itself, via the expected structure, or does it distract us through its confining labels? Yardley clearly believes the former. Lenney does, too, exclaiming that "a nonfiction writer doesn't want her reader up in the air! She doesn't want him to wonder or doubt. She has an obligation. Her job . . . is actually different from the job of a fiction writer." (Lenney et al.)

But what of the other side of the argument? Are genre categories merely contrivances to serve booksellers and publishers or act as a distraction for a reader?

Scott Nadelson, in the same AWP panel discussion Lenney participated in, weighed in. He believes that "form . . . instructs us how to situate ourselves in relation to each piece of writing we encounter." (Lenney et al.) However, he noted, that form should come from the work itself, not a genre descriptor. He expects to "let the books we read teach us how to read them." (Lenney et al.) While that might be possible in forms that are easily distinguishable (Poetry, journalism, or fantasy fiction, for example), creative nonfiction and fiction are almost indistinguishable in form. So, what then? How can we rely on the form to imply the genre if that same form serves multiple genres?

I like the way Sven Birkerts explains it:

> Genres are like etiquette: necessary for sustaining the tensions that keep things interesting. But there's another angle, I think. Everything we come up with literarily may be narrative, but we need to ask "what kind of narrative?" and "by what process?" For fiction, as traditionally conceived, invents its elements . . . while nonfiction finds its narrative, ostensibly, through discovery. So, a shapely story — a made thing — either way, but what a difference between the one and the other. (Lenney et al.)

Leslie Jamison, in a New York Times Sunday Book Review entitled "Do Genre Labels Matter Anymore?," puts another spin on the issue by making an interesting point. She believes genre labels "offer a set of crude terms we use to articulate hungers for which we haven't found or wrought a more precise vocabulary." So, genre labels are not perfect, nor are they precise, but they do help readers identify pieces of writing which will, hopefully, address a perceived literary need.

How does this apply to Wilder's writing? If genre labels provide structure, articulate hungers, display a necessary etiquette, and meet reader's expectations, then how do we categorize Wilder's hybrid work? Though she adamantly referred to it as nonfiction, we now know it was not. And I believe this knowledge has changed the way we read the *Little House* books.

When the first book was published in 1932, readers believed every word and felt a resulting intimacy with the entire Ingalls family. Wilder's assertions that it was all true reinforced this feeling of intimacy. As interest in Wilder's writings increased over time, however, bits and pieces of information surfaced which disputed or adjusted many of the stories she had told. This shifted the readers' understanding of the work from "beautifully written and true" to "beautifully written." It mattered that she had crossed genre lines.

Robynne Elizabeth Miller

NONFICTION

The books are true, you know. All those things happened to me and my parents and sisters, just as I have written them. (Wilder qtd. in Anderson 145)

"I was the Laura you have been reading about and all the books are true stories about me and my parents and sisters. All real people and things happened to them, just as I have told about in the books." (Wilder qtd. in Anderson 236)

These are bold statements for Laura Ingalls Wilder to make, especially when referring to conversations and events that happened when she was very young. But she wasn't entirely incorrect, nor did she start her writing journey with the intention to deceive. Wilder began writing her pioneer stories after her Pa, Ma, and older sister, Mary, had all passed away.

After Mary's death in 1928, Laura felt an urgent need to write her family's story, and her goal was nonfiction . . . specifically a kind of autobiography. Her intent was to preserve both her family's history as well as to chronicle an important period of America's past.

The trouble with her timing was that she was essentially elderly and alone when trying to piece together elements of the narrative. With her parents and older sister gone, she had only her two younger sisters, and a handful of elderly former neighbors and friends, to help reconstruct timelines and clarify facts. Wilder's next oldest sibling, Carrie, was more than three years younger, and their youngest sibling, Grace, was more than ten. Neither were even born when Wilder's tale begins, and were much too young to have recalled with certainty any information which would have helped in at least the first several books.

Though Wilder did a great deal of personal research to help fill in gaps, she was largely reliant on her own memory to furnish the necessary facts. And, considering the lack of access to reliable witnesses and verified accounts in the late 1920's, Wilder did a pretty decent job of constructing a mostly accurate family history. A modern survey of land records, censuses, church histories, newspaper articles, and other contemporaneous sources corroborates much of what Wilder believed was, and represented as, fact.

She was born in Pepin, Wisconsin, and her family did travel to all of the places she mentions in the books: Kansas, Walnut Grove, Silver Lake, De Smet. She had most details of her relatives correct, as well as most of the names of characters who appeared in the books (although some misspelled). She also had most of the important historical events, such as the Homestead Act, the Kansas Massacre, the Grasshopper Plague, the westward expansion of the Railroad, and the Hard Winter of 1881, placed correctly in history.

Although harder to substantiate, I believe that she wrote accurately about the personalities of her family members, too. The consistency with which she portrayed their mannerisms, speech nuances, and natures attests to this likelihood. None of the primary characters in her books, her immediate family, ever changed significantly. They grew older, they grew up, but they never grew out of their early established characters. This shows that Wilder was not constructing literary caricatures to serve some greater purpose, but merely, to the best of her ability, expressing who she believed the real people were . . . an important element of nonfiction.

Wilder's first version of her *Pioneer Girl* manuscript, from which the *Little House* books were derived, was in first person, and it covered her life from age two to eighteen. She wrote every detail, or as much as she could remember or accurately research, from her own perspective. In short, it was a memoir. But memoirs were not popular in the 1930's. Publishers, who believed that "I" stories did not sell, demanded a different perspective. Eventually, third person limited was settled on. No matter which point of view, or the genre descriptor applied, however, Wilder repeatedly asserted that her writing contained only truth.

Pamela Smith Hill, editor of "Pioneer Girl, The Annotated Autobiography," gives Wilder a little leeway on the issue. After countless hours working with Wilder's manuscripts, letters, and personal notes, Hill believes that "Pioneer Girl was nonfiction, the truth as only Wilder remembered it." (xvi) But this poses yet another important question: does something need to be factual to be considered truthful? The memoirist might say it doesn't. But in nonfiction? There is an implied contract of technical accuracy.

There is also a second contract to consider which a nonfiction writer also makes with all of their readers . . . that omissions to a story will not be made which alter the reader's full understanding of the truth. Yet, Wilder did that a number of times. During the *Long Winter*, for example, the number of townspeople present was modified, and the fact that another family (George and Maggie Masters and their newborn son, Arthur) shared the Ingalls' home, was omitted entirely. In a letter to her daughter, Rose, Wilder explains that "we can't have anyone live with us . . . or the hardships will vanish." (qtd. in Anderson 166) In another letter to Rose, Wilder states that culling real life people from the story "adds to the feeling . . . that the Ingalls family should be more of a solitary unit." (qtd. in Anderson 124). It was important to the story that the Ingalls, and the settlement, were isolated. But it was not factual.

Robynne Elizabeth Miller

MEMOIR

Because memoir is largely regarded as a subset of nonfiction, it's important to make a distinction between the two. The short answer is that they serve slightly different purposes and imbue the reader with slightly different expectations. A reader of nonfiction expects the untainted and unaltered facts of an event or time period. A reader of memoir expects a personal interpretation of that same event or period of time. Perhaps, though, we should break it down even further. Wilder's assertions that her work was factually true, and about her own life, mean it is not only nonfiction, but also an autobiography. So, how do autobiographies and memoirs connect and differ? Here are some clarifications:

> "A memoir is how one remembers one's own life, while an autobiography is history, requiring research, dates, facts double-checked" (Vidal qtd. in Best 26)

> "An autobiography focuses on the chronology of the writer's entire life while a memoir covers one specific aspect of the writer's life." (Klems)

"Unlike autobiography, which moves in a dutiful line from birth to fame, memoir narrows the lens, focusing on a time in the writer's life that was unusually vivid, such as childhood or adolescence, or that was framed by war or travel or public service or some other special circumstance" (Zinsser 15)

These definitions are all helpful in establishing the nuanced differences between nonfiction and its subset, memoir. It's true, too, that they intersect as much as they differ. They both seek to establish a truth, for example, whether factual or interpreted. They also both deal with an individual's life, and can cover similar events. While Wilder's original series spanned her life from two to eighteen, which would have been far too broad a timespan to meet the modern criteria for a memoir, she did zoom in on and process certain events in her life.

In *Little Town on the Prairie*, for example, Wilder slips into memoir when remembering an incident with a fellow schoolmate. "For a long time, Laura did not quite know what she thought about that whipping" (269) she wrote, processing the event.

> Willie was bright enough, but he had never learned his lessons. When he was called upon to recite, he let his mouth fall open and all the sense went out of his eyes. He looked less than half-witted, he hardly looked human. It made anyone sick to see him . . . Laura could not bear to see his idiot face. On the third day, Mr. Owen quietly said, "Come with me, Willie."
>
> . . . From their seat nearest the door, Ida and Laura heard the swish and thud of the pointer. Everyone heard Willie's howls.
>
> Mr. Owen came quietly in with Willie. "Stop blubbering," he said. "Go to your seat and study. I expect you to know and recite your lessons."
>
> . . . After that, one look from Mr. Owen cleared some of the idiot look from Willie's face. He seemed to be trying to think, and to act like other boys. Laura often wondered whether he could pull his mind together after he had let it go to pieces so, but at least Willie was trying. He was afraid not to try. (Wilder, *Little Town* 269)

In another book, *Little House on the Prairie*, Wilder recounts her experience with a prairie fire. The Ingalls moved to Kansas when Wilder was two and left when she was four, so this is an account through the memory of a tiny little girl. Thus, we don't just get the bare facts of event . . . we are standing with Wilder amongst the smoke and grass and ashes, as terrified as she was.

> Laura wanted to do something, but inside her head was roaring and whirling like the fire. Her middle shook, and tears poured out of her stinging eyes. Her eyes and her nose and her throat stung with smoke. (175)

When writing about Wilder's original manuscript, *Pioneer Girl*, which Wilder first wrote in the late 1920's, Pamela Smith Hill noted that "this story was personal, a memoir about Wilder's past and her family's unique pioneering experience" (xvi). She explains further:

> *I lay and looked.* This phrase signals that Pioneer Girl is a memoir, Wilder's personal narrative of her childhood and adolescence. Memoirs, by their nature, are written in first-person, from the author's unique and personal perspective. In *Pioneer Girl*, Wilder conveyed her memories, impressions, and feelings directly, in her own voice, using the "I" pronoun. Wilder's novels, however, employed a different point of view—third person limited. (3)

It's important to note that all of the *Little House* books were derived from that first manuscript, which was a memoir, and some historians still want to categorize the resulting series as memoir, as well. After all, from *Pioneer Girl*, we know that memoir is where Wilder's initial writing instincts took her and where her emotional reactions to her own story lay. *Pioneer Girl* was also the fleshed-out project from which she "lifted" numerous portions of text, laden with emotion and introspection. Publishers may have convinced her to modify her manuscript to be more suitable for children, but Wilder never strayed from wanting to write the stories of her heart.

If Wilder *was* writing a memoir through the *Little House* series, at least in part, what responsibility did she have to insure the story's accuracy? Two essays, "Memory and Imagination" by Patricia Hampl and "Memoir? Fiction? Where's the Line?" by Mimi Schwartz wrestle with a tricky literary issue that is pertinent to the discussion of Wilder's work: how much truth is required when you are writing memoir?

Schwartz believes that "if the main plot, characters, and setting are true, if the intent is to make honest sense of 'how it felt to me' and tell that true story well (with disclaimers as needed), it's memoir." (qtd. in Root 411) Schwartz appreciates and honors the writer's attempt "to explore the emotional truth of a memory." (qtd. in Root 411) To that end, and despite some mixed portions of fiction and autobiographical fact, she might therefore applaud Wilder's hybrid effort as a whole. Schwartz has no problem fictionalizing minor details to emphasize a truth. And that is precisely what Wilder did. In emphasizing and calling out the larger narrative arc she was serving, facts blurred, timelines rearranged, and characters appeared or disappeared. But we mostly knew how Wilder felt about the events she was portraying. Not factually true, but the greater story was well served.

Hampl, on the other hand, thinks that "a reader has a right to expect a memoir to be as accurate as the writer's memory can make it." (qtd. in Root 334) So, if Wilder knowingly omitted or shaped facts to suit her larger purpose, Hampl would likely call her on it.

Especially if she also presented the work as factual.

In the end, I agree with both. A memoir should be an attempt to "explore the emotional truth of a memory," but it should also be firmly rooted in facts. Schwartz states that "you have to play by the rules. There's a line you can't cross" and "if you make up too much, you've crossed it."

There is a case to be made that Wilder "made too much up." Besides the pure fiction of many scenes and characters, she also recounted conversations she could not have heard or remembered, changed timelines to smooth the story out, and eliminated details which lessened the drama she was trying to convey. But to what end? Did it affect our reading of her story or our response to it? Wilder crossed all sorts of lines . . . she stuck to pure facts at some points, delved into the emotions of scenes at others, and made up a number of things throughout the series.

Omitting unnecessary details or slightly re-shaping a story so that the emotional resonance is unclouded and well-defined is acceptable to me. But only if you are calling your work a memoir. Wilder did not, and there is the difficult part. Her work contained pure fiction.

FICTION

The act of fictionalizing what is presented as
autobiography or memoir
continues to be controversial. (Hill 355)

Three stories in the *Little House* series always stuck out to me in particular. One was the moment Pa decided to leave his homestead in Kansas. "I'll not stay here to be taken away by the soldiers like an outlaw!" Pa declared. (Wilder, *Little House on the Prairie* 198) I was heartbroken for the family, who'd worked so hard to establish a home and farm on the bare, isolated prairie, and angry that Pa had been given wrong information about the land being open to settlement. It wasn't fair!

The second story was about the time Mr. Edwards helped Pa thwart a whole crowd of desperate, bullying settlers who were trying to keep Pa from filing a claim. "Go in, Ingalls! I'll fix 'im! Yow-ee-ee!" Mr. Edwards exclaimed, landing on the backs of the worst two, and diverting the fight so Pa could get into the land office and file. (Wilder, *Silver Lake* 236) The crowd frightened me, but it was just like beloved Mr. Edwards to appear in the nick of time and save the day!

The third story that deeply affected me was the gut-wrenching scene where Jack, the Ingalls' beloved bulldog, died on the banks of Plum Creek. Friend, protector, and companion, Jack had been a loyal member of the family throughout their crisscrossing of the prairie in search of a permanent home. I cried and cried as they found "Jack's body, stiff and cold" (Wilder, *Silver Lake* 12) and then buried him on a low slope above the wheat field in Walnut Grove.

But I shouldn't have. Cried, I mean. That story, and the others, were pure fiction. To be honest, when I realized this as a young adult, I felt manipulated and deeply disappointed. Though I didn't know or understand the implications of genre labels, and their corresponding expectations, at that age, I did understand the concept of "truth." Wilder had represented the books as factually accurate. But, yet, here I learned that they were really a blend of truth and fiction. The contract, in my mind, had been broken. And my reading of the novels had been fractured.

I had no problem with Wilder not remembering an historic conversation verbatim, and simply relating to us the gist, instead. Nor did I mind a judicious removal of characters or occasional condensing of timelines. But outright fiction in a work touted as truth was, and is, a bit of an ethical stretch. Mr. Edwards (and there's much controversy over whether he was a real person in the first place) never helped Pa file a claim. The Kansas homestead wasn't as isolated as Wilder made it out, and plenty of neighbors stayed after the Ingalls left, without soldiers appearing. So it wasn't the certainty of being removed that drove their decision to leave . . . it was likelier the fact that the buyer for their Pepin cabin had defaulted on his payments and the Ingalls wanted to return home. Worst of all, however, was that Jack never made it to Walnut Grove. He stayed back in Pepin with a pair of horses Pa had traded. Jack preferred those horses to the family. So his loyalty to the family and the whole death scene was pure, excruciating fiction.

Wilder once wrote a letter about the Mr. Edwards/claim filing story. She justified her use of fiction by saying:

> As to the place where homesteads were filed,
> that chapter is fiction. Such things did happen
> in those days and I placed it there to
> emphasize the rush for land. You understand
> how those things are done in writing. (qtd. in
> Anderson 211)

In another letter, Wilder is speaking of her book
These Happy Golden Years. "Like the others, this book
is true to facts, with touches of fiction here and there to
help the interest." (qtd. in Anderson 242)

As a narrative decision, I think these stories
were brilliant additions. Through them, Wilder
highlighted everything from the rush for homestead
land, the political climate during westward expansion,
and even the inevitable losses life on the prairie
included. They were not factual, but they were true to
the greater pioneer story.

But the addition of these fictitious stories to the
series, especially under the category of nonfiction, puts
the rest of Wilder's work on shaky ground. If these
emotive stories were not true, what else wasn't? For the

modern writer, Wilder's decision to blend genres provides a weighty caution. We risk losing the trust and fidelity of our readers if we label something as nonfiction, but are proven to be false. Isn't it better to claim fiction, with truth sprinkled throughout, rather than the other way around?

Wilder didn't think so, at least in the beginning. When fans asked about the stories, she would uphold their supposed truth. With her own daughter, Rose, however, the reality was evident. In that collaboration, "Wilder discusses the fabrication of the novels' recurring neighbor character, Mr. Edwards, and explains the creation of her nemesis Nellie Oleson as a composite, modeled after a few different girls from her childhood. But to fans she maintained the fiction." (Liebenthal)

The lasting question, however, is why she chose to move into the realm of fiction. Here's one possibility:

> For centuries writers of nonfiction have borrowed the tools of novelists to reveal truths

that could be exposed and rendered in no better way. They place characters in scenes and settings, have them speak to each other in dialogue, reveal limited points of view, and move through time over conflicts and toward resolutions. (Clark)

Wilder's first book, *Little House in the Big Woods*, wasn't about the westward movement or the Homestead Act or the sturdy pioneers. It was basically a year in the life of a mid- to late-1880's family. They made butter, smoked meats, chinked their cabin, and stored food for winter. It was the story of Wilder's childhood.

But the stories quickly began to be larger than the Ingalls' personal narrative. In the second book of the series, *Little House on the Prairie*, the story of the Ingalls begins to mingle with the stories of other homesteaders pushing west, as well as the larger American frontier narrative of the time. While Wilder did use some creative nonfiction techniques, such as dialog and scenes, in *Little House in the Big Woods*, the book, though a charming snapshot of 1800's backwoods living, had no universal implication. But in

Little House on the Prairie, the larger story of America's pioneer movement began to overtake Wilder's simple family history, and fiction began to creep into her work. Mr. Edwards, for example, is at best, a semi-fictitious character and, at worst, pure fiction. The reason that Pa left Kansas, however, was almost certainly not for the reasons the book stated. These were only a couple of examples of "truth-stretching," but it was the beginning. As the novels progressed, fiction became more and more prevalent in the weave of her narration. Timelines were condensed and shifted. Characters were omitted, added, or made into composites. Stories were invented. Details were altered.

Why? Because there was a shift of purpose from the first book through the series. By the end, her own family's story was simply a vehicle through which to address the greater themes Wilder was interested in: self-reliance, homesteading, America's westward expansion. Though she was intending to tell the truth of her family when she began, as the story developed, Wilder became more interested in telling the truth of the period in history than she was in creating a factual account of her family's history. Clark would assert that she had to incorporate fiction into the narrative . . . for the pioneer story could "be exposed and rendered in no better way."

CONCLUSION

There is no doubt that Wilder primarily worked with facts. Censuses, letters, land records, and other contemporaneous evidence corroborate the lion's share of *Little House* details. But it's also indisputable that some of what Wilder wrote was pure fiction. She, herself, eventually admitted to this, and modern research has substantiated it. There's also no denying that portions of the creative nonfiction narrative Wilder established slipped over the line into memoir. But to what effect? And what can other writers learn from Wilder's hybrid genre?

Wilder is a unique case. Her stories are so endearing, and so beautifully written, that many readers are willing to give her a "pass" on fudged details. She also enjoys an international audience, having published in sixty countries, and have her work translated into over forty languages. Most of those international readers are far more concerned with a peek into 1800's America than with the Ingalls, specifically. And, of course, to be blunt, she's dead. It's difficult to be too accusing of a woman who published in her dotage, between the ages of sixty-five and seventy-five, and who is no longer here to defend her writing.

Do modern writers enjoy those same conditions? Of course not. Therefore, the bar is higher for us. We live in an age where fact-checking is often as easy as flipping on your computer or making a phone call. We don't have the outpouring of unconditional love from tens of millions of fans. We aren't, for the most part, writing about an idealized portion of American history, nor have we lived through it. And, if we're reading this, we're not dead. Expecting the same grace and leniency from a modern audience is out.

That doesn't mean we cannot blend genres, however. We can. And there is much to be learned from Wilder's understanding of narrative arc and how to embellish a story so that it serves the greater purpose and theme of a story. She added drama with the tale of Pa filing his claim, which illuminated the frenzy of the land rush. She added drama with the story of being kicked out of Kansas, which highlighted the issues with national communication, Indian territories, and the fervor of pioneers pushing west. She added drama with the death of Jack, bringing in a palatable touch of the harsh realities of frontier life.

Yet, despite her success, we must be honest when we are blending genres, or risk breaking trust with our audience. Wilder got away with it, but I submit that modern writers would not.

Robynne Elizabeth Miller

WORKS CITED

Best, John. *A Professor at the End of Time: The Work and Future of the Professoriate*. Rutgers UP, 17 Mar. 2017.

Clark, Roy Peter. "The Line Between Fact and Fiction." Poynter Institute, 30 June, 2002, http://www.poynter.org/2002/the-line-between-fact-and-fiction/1500/. Accessed 15 Apr. 2017.

Hill, Pamela Smith, editor. *Pioneer Girl: The Annotated Autobiography*. South Dakota Historical Soc. Press, 2014.

Jamison, Leslie. "Do Genre Labels Matter Anymore?" *New York Times*, 30 June 2015, www.nytimes.com/2015/07/05/books/review/do-genre-labels-matter-anymore.html?_r=2. Accessed 15 Mar. 2017.

Klems, Brian A. "Memoir vs. Autobiography." *Writer's Digest*, 8 May 2013, www.writersdigest.com/online-editor/memoir-vs-autobiography-2. Accessed 1 Apr. 2017.

Laube, Steve. "Does Genre Matter?" 29 June 2015, stevelaube.com/does-genre-matter/. Accessed 11 Mar. 2017.

Lenney, Dinah, et al. "Why Genre Matters." *Los Angeles Review of Books*, 23 Aug. 2013, lareviewofbooks.org/article/why-genre-matters/. Accessed 15 Mar. 2017.

Liebenthal, Ryann. "Our Lady of the Plains." 2 Mar. 2016, newrepublic.com/article/129021/laura-ingalls-wilder. Accessed 10 Mar. 2017.

Root, Robert L. *The Fourth Genre: Contemporary Writers of/on Creative Nonfiction.* Pearson Education, Inc., 2010.

Yardley, Cathy. "Why Genre Matters." *Writer Unboxed*, 30 Sept. 2014, writerunboxed.com/2014/09/30/why-genre-matters/. Accessed 16 Mar. 2017.

Wilder, Laura Ingalls. *By the Shores of Silver Lake.* 1939. Full Color ed., HarperTrophy, 2004.

---. *The First Four Years.* 1971. HarperTrophy, 1972.

---. *Little House in the Big Woods.* 1932. HarperTrophy, 1971.

---. *Little House on the Prairie*. 1935. Mammoth, 1994.

---. *Little Town on the Prairie*. HarperTrophy, 1971.

---. *The Long Winter*. 1940. Puffin Books, 1968.

---. *On the Banks of Plum Creek*. 1937. Mammoth, 1994.

---. *These Happy Golden Years*. 1941. HarperCollins, 2008.

Zinsser, William. *Inventing the Truth: The Art and Craft of Memoir*. Mariner Books, 20 May 1998.

MISCELLANEOUS QUOTES ON THE TOPIC

"Author Lawrence Weschler once said, "Every narrative voice — and especially every nonfiction narrative voice — is a fiction. And the world of writing and reading is divided into those who know this and those who don't." ~ Dinah Lenney

"People have been writing autobiographical fiction for just about ever — and blurring genre boundaries, too. But if you don't clue us in, if we find out after the fact, it's a one-sided game, isn't it? In which case, you're all alone on the seesaw. Does that sound like fun? Does that sound like art? If so, okay — but whoever you are, you're not writing nonfiction. Because a nonfiction writer doesn't want her reader up in the air! She doesn't want him to wonder or doubt. She has an obligation. Her job — that is my job — is actually different from the job of a fiction writer. And I want my reader to believe he can count on me to revel in its challenges and rewards." ~Dinah Lenney

In a recent essay/review in The New Republic, critic Adam Kirsch observed: "The essayist is concerned, as a fiction writer is not, with what the reader will think of him or her."

"even the most well-researched book is full of omissions and bias and human limitation." ~Scott Nadelson

I think of "fiction" etymologically — and we shouldn't forget our etymologies — as a "made thing." And nonfiction is a "made thing" as well. And maybe this is where some of the confusion originates. ~Sven Birkerts

The beauty of fiction is that it frees us from wondering about the messy status of things, people, and events so that we can give ourselves completely to their purposeful interaction. ~Sven Birkerts

Both processes [of writing fiction and nonfiction] are determined significantly by the sensibility, the psychological character, of the writer, but the actions mark the difference between essentially opposite kinds of agency. Fiction says "let it be the case that" and nonfiction says, in whatever uniquely subjective way, "it is the case that." ~Sven Birkerts

In fiction we must contend with the author's intention first and foremost . . . In nonfiction we must contend with the merger of the author's actual psyche and the actual world, and ask not so much why this version of things, as how? How did this account arise from this person, these givens? Our attention is, at the deepest readerly level, directed at different things. There is nothing gained whatsoever in trying to get them to be the same thing. ~Sven Birkerts

Why are autobiography and biography separated as categories? Would one category called, say, "lives," do the trick? Though: would deeply researched biography, say, of the Robert Caro variety have a necessary edge over the private confessional memoir, or what you will, say, of the Mary Karr variety? ~David Biespiel

Clive James, author of the memoir, Unreliable Memoirs, some of which is not true, puts it this way. Memoirs that dramatize "conceal more than they reveal." He writes: [My] first volume, Unreliable Memoirs, has been a very good friend to me, especially in Britain and Australia. It's never caught on in America. It's because I say right at the start, "Some of this isn't true." You can't do that in America . . . In America, the label has to say what's in the can, so in the supermarket you know what you're picking up. ~David Biespiel

"When I was writing an essay, I was hoping to discover what that memory meant, how it was relevant to the person I am today. I was looking to what I could make of my life and the forces that shaped it." ~Judith Kitchen

Reverse the process. There's no way for the reader to know what is real, what imagined. Only I know why I choose to call one thing nonfiction and the other fiction. But I do choose. ~Judith Kitchen

Nonfiction is built on a scaffold of fact. Even the essay, with its greater leeway for exploration and play owes its fidelity to the facts. Its purpose is self-knowledge, not self-invention. The real invention is the speaking voice. ~Judith Kitchen

In fiction, the writer recedes and we repress our own experience in favor of what is happening to the characters. Events matter to the reader directly, from inside. Time itself is liberated, and the book lives on in a continuous present. ~Judith Kitchen

And that's why genre matters. Without nonfiction, fiction is dead. In an ironic reversal of roles, nonfiction provides us with an alternative self by which to make comparisons. ~Judith Kitchen

What if we thought of genre in this way, as a set of groping terms seeking the contours of more nebulous hungers? What if genre was just desire in the dark? It seems to me that genre labels are just a way of making small talk at the picnic, which only mattered — in the end — as prelude to the more complicated years of conversation that followed. ~ Leslie Jamison

ABOUT THE AUTHOR

Robynne Elizabeth Miller has authored numerous nonfiction books, articles, and essays, mostly relating to pioneer life or the *Little House on the Prairie* series. An experienced speaker, editor, and writing coach, Robynne also teaches at writers conferences and local writers workshops. She leads two writing/critique groups, volunteers with West Coast Christian Writers, and is the Director of Leadership for the Inspire Christian Writers board of directors.

Robynne lives with her British husband and the youngest two of their four wonderful children in the snowy woods of the Sierra Nevada Mountains of Northern California. When not writing, Robynne loves singing, felling trees, and making bacon from scratch.

Robynne Elizabeth Miller

OTHER BOOKS BY THE AUTHOR

Slightly Strange SAVORY Pioneer Recipes
(that actually taste good!)

Slightly Strange SWEET Pioneer Recipes
(that are delicious!)

Super Simple SAVORY Pioneer Recipes
(five ingredients or less!)

Super Easy SWEET Pioneer Recipes
(five ingredients or less!)

From the Mouth of Ma
A Search for Caroline Quiner Ingalls

Pioneer Mixology
A quirky survey (with recipes!) of pioneer beverages

The Three Faces of Nellie
An in-depth biography of the three women who made up the composite *Little House* character of Nellie Oleson.

CONTACT

Email

robynne@robynnemiller.com

Web

robynnemiller.com

mylittleprairiehome.com & thepracticalpioneer.com

Twitter

@mlprairiehome

Pinterest

pinterest.com/mlprairiehome/

Facebook

www.facebook.com/robynneelizabethmiller/

www.ingramcontent.com/pod-product-compliance
Lightning Source LLC
Chambersburg PA
CBHW021222020426
42331CB00003B/425